Pressure Cooker Beef Stew Cookbook

Delicious and Time-Saving Recipes for Hearty Beef Stews Made Effortlessly in Your Pressure Cooker

PRESSURE COOKER BEEF STEW COOKBOOK

First edition. January 24, 2024.

Copyright © 2024 john ahmad.

ISBN: 979-8224849123

Written by john ahmad.

Table of Contents

John Ahmad

Chapter 1: Introduction to Pressure Cooking

Pressure cooking is a game-changer in the kitchen, allowing you to prepare delicious meals in a fraction of the time. In this chapter, we will explore the benefits of pressure cooking, help you become familiar with your pressure cooker, and provide essential tips and safety guidelines to ensure a successful cooking experience.

1.1 Benefits of Pressure Cooking

Pressure cooking offers numerous advantages that make it a must-have tool in your kitchen arsenal. Here are some of the key benefits:

Timesaving: With the ability to cook meals up to 70% faster than traditional methods, pressure cooking is perfect for busy individuals and families.

Retains nutrients: The sealed environment of a pressure cooker helps to preserve the nutrients in your ingredients, ensuring healthier and more nutritious meals.

Enhanced flavors: The high-pressure environment in a cooker allows flavors to infuse more deeply, resulting in rich and robust dishes.

Tenderizes tough cuts of meat: Pressure cooking breaks down the collagen in tougher cuts of meat, making them incredibly tender and succulent.

Energy-efficient: The shorter cooking time and reduced need for multiple pots and pans make pressure cooking an energy-saving option.

Versatile: From soups and stews to grains and desserts, a pressure cooker can handle a wide range of recipes and ingredients.

1.2 Getting Familiar with Your Pressure Cooker

Before diving into recipes, it's important to understand the components and functions of your pressure cooker. Here are the key elements to familiarize yourself with:

Lid and sealing ring: The lid is a crucial part of the pressure cooker, and it usually has a sealing ring that ensures airtight cooking.

Pressure release valve: This valve controls the pressure levels inside the cooker. It can be manual or automatic, depending on the model.

Pressure indicator: The pressure indicator shows the pressure level inside the cooker, indicating when it has reached the desired level.

Cooking pot: The cooking pot is where you'll place your ingredients for cooking. It is often made of stainless steel or non-stick material.

Handles and safety features: Pressure cookers have handles for easy handling and safety features like locking mechanisms and pressure release systems to prevent accidents.

1.3 Essential Tips and Safety Guidelines

To ensure a safe and successful pressure-cooking experience, here are some essential tips and guidelines to keep in mind:

Read the manual: Familiarize yourself with the specific instructions and safety guidelines provided by the manufacturer of your pressure cooker.

Use enough liquid: Always ensure that you have sufficient liquid in the cooker to generate the necessary steam and maintain the pressure.

Don't overfill: Leave enough headspace in the cooker to allow the contents to expand during cooking. Check the maximum fill line indicated in your cooker.

Release pressure safely: Follow the recommended methods for releasing pressure, whether it's natural release, quick release, or a combination of both.

Clean and maintain your cooker: Regularly clean the various parts of your pressure cooker according to the manufacturer's instructions to ensure its longevity.

Experiment and have fun: Pressure cooking may take some practices, so don't be afraid to experiment with different recipes and techniques to find your favorites.

By understanding the benefits, components, and safety guidelines of pressure cooking, you're now ready to embark on a flavorful and time-saving culinary journey. In the upcoming chapters, we will explore a variety of mouthwatering beef stew recipes that will become your go-to meals in no time. Let's get cooking!

Chapter 2: Beef Stew Basics

To create a delicious and hearty beef stew, it's important to start with a solid foundation. In this chapter, we will delve into the fundamentals of beef stew, including understanding the different cuts of beef for stewing, tips for selecting the best ingredients, and essential spices and flavorings that will elevate your stew to new heights of flavor.

2.1 Understanding the Different Cuts of Beef for Stewing

Choosing the right cut of beef is essential for a tender and flavorful stew. Here are some popular cuts that work well for stewing:

Chuck: This cut comes from the shoulder region of the cow and is marbled with fat, which adds richness and tenderness to the stew.

Brisket: Known for its exceptional flavor, brisket is a tough but highly rewarding cut when cooked low and slow in a stew.

Shank: The shank cut contains a lot of connective tissue, which breaks down during the stewing process, resulting in a gelatinous and flavorful stew.

Short Ribs: These meaty and well-marbled ribs are perfect for adding depth of flavor to your stew. They require longer cooking times but are worth the wait.

Round: The round cuts, such as bottom round or eye of round, are leaner and can be used for a leaner and healthier beef stew.

2.2 Tips for Selecting the Best Ingredients

Besides choosing the right cut of beef, selecting fresh and high-quality ingredients will enhance the overall taste of your beef stew. Here are some tips for ingredient selection:

Fresh vegetables: opt for fresh, seasonal vegetables such as carrots, onions, celery, and potatoes. They add texture, flavor, and nutrients to your stew.

Aromatics: Garlic and herbs like thyme, rosemary, and bay leaves infuse the stew with fragrant and savory notes.

Stock or broth: Choose a good-quality beef stock or broth to build a flavorful base for your stew. Alternatively, you can make your own homemade stock for added depth of flavor.

Wine or beer: Adding a splash of red wine or dark beer can further enhance the richness and complexity of your beef stew.

Seasonings: Don't forget to season your stew with salt and pepper to bring out the flavors of the ingredients.

2.3 Essential Spices and Flavorings for Beef Stew

Spices and flavorings play a crucial role in elevating the taste profile of your beef stew. Here are some essential spices and flavorings to consider:

Paprika: This smoky and slightly sweet spice adds depth and a rich red color to your stew.

Cumin: A warm and earthy spice that complements beef and adds complexity to the overall flavor profile.

Worcestershire sauce: A few dashes of Worcestershire sauce bring a tangy and savory note to your stew.

Tomato paste: Adding tomato paste provides a depth of umami flavor and helps thicken the stew.

Balsamic vinegar: A splash of balsamic vinegar adds a touch of acidity and sweetness to balance the richness of the beef.

Experiment with different combinations of spices and flavorings to find your preferred flavor profile. Remember to taste and adjust the seasonings as you go.

By understanding the different cuts of beef for stewing, selecting high-quality ingredients, and utilizing essential spices and flavorings, you're equipped with the knowledge to create a mouthwatering beef stew. In the next chapters, we'll dive into specific recipes that showcase the versatility and deliciousness of this classic dish. Get ready to savor the flavors of your homemade beef stews!

Chapter 3: Classic Beef Stews

In this chapter, we'll explore three timeless and beloved classic beef stew recipes. These comforting dishes have stood the test of time and continue to delight with their rich flavors and hearty textures. Get ready to savor the warmth and nostalgia of traditional beef stew with root vegetables, indulge in the robust flavors of Guinness beef stew, and experience the elegance of French-style beef bourguignon.

3.1 Traditional Beef Stew with Root Vegetables
Ingredients:

- 2 pounds (900g) beef chuck, cut into 1-inch cubes
- 2 tablespoons olive oil
- 1 onion, chopped
- 3 cloves garlic, minced
- 2 carrots, peeled and cut into chunks
- 2 parsnips, peeled and cut into chunks
- 2 potatoes, peeled and cut into chunks
- 2 celery stalks, sliced
- 4 cups beef broth
- 1 cup red wine
- 2 tablespoons tomato paste
- 2 bay leaves
- 1 teaspoon dried thyme
- Salt and pepper to taste
- Chopped fresh parsley for garnish

Instructions:

1. Heat the olive oil in a large Dutch oven or a pressure cooker

over medium-high heat. Brown the beef cubes on all sides until nicely seared. Remove the beef from the pot and set aside.

2. In the same pot, add the chopped onion and minced garlic. Sauté until fragrant and golden.

3. Add the carrots, parsnips, potatoes, and celery to the pot. Cook for a few minutes, stirring occasionally.

4. Return the seared beef to the pot. Pour in the beef broth and red wine, followed by the tomato paste. Stir well to combine.

5. Add the bay leaves and dried thyme. Season with salt and pepper to taste.

6. If using a pressure cooker, secure the lid and cook on high pressure for 25 minutes. For a stovetop method, simmer the stew covered for 2-3 hours until the beef is tender and the flavors have melded together.

Once cooked, remove the bay leaves and adjust the seasoning if needed. Serve the traditional beef stew hot, garnished with freshly chopped parsley. Enjoy with crusty bread or over a bed of fluffy mashed potatoes.

3.2 Hearty Guinness Beef Stew

Ingredients:

- 2 pounds (900g) beef stew meat, cut into chunks
- 3 tablespoons all-purpose flour
- Salt and pepper to taste
- 3 tablespoons olive oil
- 1 onion, chopped
- 3 cloves garlic, minced
- 2 carrots, peeled and sliced
- 2 celery stalks, sliced
- 1 can (14.9 oz/440ml) Guinness beer
- 2 cups beef broth
- 2 tablespoons tomato paste
- 2 bay leaves
- 1 teaspoon dried thyme
- 1 tablespoon Worcestershire sauce
- Chopped fresh parsley for garnish

Instructions:

1. In a bowl, combine the flour, salt, and pepper. Toss the beef chunks in the flour mixture until coated evenly.
2. Heat the olive oil in a Dutch oven or a pressure cooker over medium-high heat. Brown the beef chunks on all sides until nicely seared. Remove the beef from the pot and set aside.
3. In the same pot, add the chopped onion and minced garlic. Sauté until softened and fragrant.
4. Add the carrots and celery to the pot, cooking for a few minutes until slightly tender.
5. Return the seared beef to the pot. Pour in the Guinness beer and beef broth, followed by the tomato paste. Stir well to combine.

6. Add the bay leaves, dried thyme, and Worcestershire sauce. Season with salt and pepper to taste.
7. If using a pressure cooker, secure the lid and cook on high pressure for 25 minutes. For a stovetop method, simmer the stew covered for 2-3 hours until the beef is tender and the flavors have melded together.

Once cooked, remove the bay leaves and adjust the seasoning if needed. Serve the hearty Guinness beef stew hot, garnished with freshly chopped parsley. Pair it with a slice of Irish soda bread for a complete meal.

3.3 French-Style Beef Bourguignon
Ingredients:

- 2 pounds (900g) beef chuck, cut into 1-inch cubes
- 4 tablespoons all-purpose flour
- Salt and pepper to taste
- 4 tablespoons olive oil
- 6 slices bacon, chopped
- 1 onion, chopped
- 4 cloves garlic, minced
- 2 carrots, peeled and sliced
- 10-12 pearl onions, peeled
- 1 pound (450g) mushrooms, quartered
- 2 cups red wine (preferably Burgundy)
- 2 cups beef broth
- 2 tablespoons tomato paste
- 2 bay leaves
- 1 teaspoon dried thyme
- Chopped fresh parsley for garnish

Instructions:

1. In a bowl, combine the flour, salt, and pepper. Toss the beef cubes in the flour mixture until coated evenly.
2. Heat the olive oil in a Dutch oven or a pressure cooker over medium-high heat. Brown the beef cubes on all sides until nicely seared. Remove the beef from the pot and set aside.
3. In the same pot, add the chopped bacon and cook until crispy. Remove the bacon with a slotted spoon and set aside, leaving the bacon fat in the pot.
4. Add the chopped onion and minced garlic to the pot. Sauté until golden and fragrant.
5. Add the carrots, pearl onions, and mushrooms to the pot. Cook

for a few minutes until slightly tender.

6. Return the seared beef and cooked bacon to the pot. Pour in the red wine and beef broth, followed by the tomato paste. Stir well to combine.

7. Add the bay leaves and dried thyme. Season with salt and pepper to taste.

8. If using a pressure cooker, secure the lid and cook on high pressure for 25 minutes. For a stovetop method, simmer the stew covered for 2-3 hours until the beef is tender and the flavors have melded together.

Once cooked, remove the bay leaves and adjust the seasoning if needed. Serve the French-style beef bourguignon hot, garnished with freshly chopped parsley. Enjoy with a side of crusty baguette or buttered noodles.

These classic beef stew recipes will fill your home with irresistible aromas and bring comfort to your table. In the next chapters, we'll explore creative twists and international flavors inspired by beef stews from around the world. Get ready to expand your culinary horizons and discover new favorites!

Chapter 4: Exotic Flavor Infusions

In this chapter, we'll take a culinary journey to explore exotic flavor infusions in beef stews. These recipes will introduce you to the vibrant and tantalizing flavors of Mexican, Indian, and Thai cuisines. Get ready to spice things up with a fiery Mexican-inspired beef stew, indulge in the fragrant and aromatic spices of Indian beef curry stew, and savor the delicate balance of flavors in a Thai-style lemongrass-infused beef stew.

4.1 Spicy Mexican-Inspired Beef Stew
Ingredients:

- 2 pounds (900g) beef stew meat, cut into chunks
- 3 tablespoons olive oil
- 1 onion, chopped
- 3 cloves garlic, minced
- 1 jalapeño pepper, seeded and chopped
- 1 red bell pepper, chopped
- 2 tomatoes, chopped
- 2 cups beef broth
- 1 cup tomato sauce
- 2 teaspoons chili powder
- 1 teaspoon ground cumin
- 1 teaspoon dried oregano
- Salt and pepper to taste
- Fresh cilantro for garnish
- Lime wedges for serving

Instructions:

1. Heat the olive oil in a Dutch oven or a pressure cooker over medium-high heat. Brown the beef chunks on all sides until nicely seared. Remove the beef from the pot and set aside.

2. In the same pot, add the chopped onion, minced garlic, jalapeño pepper, and red bell pepper. Sauté until the vegetables are softened.
3. Add the chopped tomatoes to the pot and cook for a few minutes until they begin to break down.
4. Return the seared beef to the pot. Pour in the beef broth and tomato sauce. Stir well to combine.
5. Add the chili powder, ground cumin, dried oregano, salt, and pepper. Stir to evenly distribute the spices.
6. If using a pressure cooker, secure the lid and cook on high pressure for 25 minutes. For a stovetop method, simmer the stew covered for 2-3 hours until the beef is tender and the flavors have melded together.

Once cooked, adjust the seasoning if needed. Serve the spicy Mexican-inspired beef stew hot, garnished with fresh cilantro. Squeeze lime juice over each serving for an extra burst of tanginess. Enjoy with warm tortillas or rice.

4.2 Fragrant Indian Beef Curry Stew
Ingredients:

- 2 pounds (900g) beef stew meat, cut into chunks
- 3 tablespoons vegetable oil
- 1 onion, finely chopped
- 3 cloves garlic, minced
- 1 tablespoon fresh ginger, grated
- 2 teaspoons ground cumin
- 2 teaspoons ground coriander
- 1 teaspoon turmeric
- 1/2 teaspoon cayenne pepper (adjust to taste)
- 1 cinnamon stick
- 2 tomatoes, chopped
- 1 cup beef broth
- 1 cup coconut milk
- Salt to taste
- Chopped fresh cilantro for garnish

Instructions:

1. Heat the vegetable oil in a Dutch oven or a pressure cooker over medium-high heat. Brown the beef chunks on all sides until nicely seared. Remove the beef from the pot and set aside.
2. In the same pot, add the chopped onion and sauté until golden brown.
3. Add the minced garlic and grated ginger to the pot. Cook for another minute until fragrant.
4. Add the ground cumin, ground coriander, turmeric, cayenne pepper, and cinnamon stick to the pot. Stir and cook for a minute to toast the spices.
5. Return the seared beef to the pot. Add the chopped tomatoes, beef broth, and coconut milk. Stir well to combine.

6. If using a pressure cooker, secure the lid and cook on high pressure for 25 minutes. For a stovetop method, simmer the stew covered for 2-3 hours until the beef is tender and the flavors have melded together.

Once cooked, season with salt to taste. Serve the fragrant Indian beef curry stew hot, garnished with fresh cilantro. Pair it with steamed basmati rice or naan bread to soak up the flavorful sauce.

4.3 Thai-Style Lemongrass-Infused Beef Stew
Ingredients:

- 2 pounds (900g) beef stew meat, cut into chunks
- 3 tablespoons vegetable oil
- 1 onion, chopped
- 3 cloves garlic, minced
- 1 stalk lemongrass, trimmed and bruised
- 1 red bell pepper, sliced
- 1 cup sliced mushrooms
- 2 tablespoons fish sauce
- 2 tablespoons soy sauce
- 1 tablespoon brown sugar
- 1 can (14 oz/400ml) coconut milk
- 2 cups beef broth
- 1 tablespoon lime juice
- Fresh cilantro and sliced red chili for garnish

Instructions:

1. Heat the vegetable oil in a Dutch oven or a pressure cooker over medium-high heat. Brown the beef chunks on all sides until nicely seared. Remove the beef from the pot and set aside.
2. In the same pot, add the chopped onion and sauté until translucent.
3. Add the minced garlic and bruised lemongrass stalk to the pot. Cook for a minute until fragrant.
4. Return the seared beef to the pot. Add the sliced red bell pepper and mushrooms.
5. In a bowl, whisk together the fish sauce, soy sauce, brown sugar, coconut milk, and beef broth. Pour the mixture into the pot and stir well to combine.
6. If using a pressure cooker, secure the lid and cook on high

pressure for 25 minutes. For a stovetop method, simmer the stew covered for 2-3 hours until the beef is tender and the flavors have melded together.

7. Once cooked, remove the lemongrass stalk. Stir in the lime juice. Adjust the seasoning if needed.

8. Serve the Thai-style lemongrass-infused beef stew hot, garnished with fresh cilantro and sliced red chili. Enjoy it with steamed jasmine rice or noodles for a complete Thai dining experience.

These exotic flavor-infused beef stew recipes will transport your taste buds to new culinary horizons. In the next chapters, we'll explore innovative twists and lighter variations of beef stew that cater to different dietary preferences. Get ready to expand your repertoire and discover even more delicious possibilities!

Chapter 5: Comforting Slow-Cooked Stews

In this chapter, we'll dive into the world of comforting slow-cooked stews. These recipes are perfect for those lazy weekends or when you want to enjoy the delightful aroma filling your home while the flavors meld together over hours of gentle cooking. Get ready to savor the melt-in-your-mouth slow-cooked pot roast stew, indulge in the tender braised beef stew with red wine, and enjoy the rustic charm of a beef and barley stew.

5.1 Slow-Cooked Pot Roast Stew

Ingredients:

- 3 pounds (1.4kg) beef chuck roast
- Salt and pepper to taste
- 2 tablespoons olive oil
- 1 onion, chopped
- 3 cloves garlic, minced
- 4 carrots, peeled and sliced
- 3 celery stalks, sliced
- 2 cups beef broth
- 1 cup red wine
- 2 tablespoons tomato paste
- 2 bay leaves
- 1 teaspoon dried thyme
- 1 teaspoon dried rosemary
- 1 pound (450g) baby potatoes, halved
- Chopped fresh parsley for garnish

Instructions:

1. Season the beef chuck roast with salt and pepper on all sides.

2. Heat the olive oil in a large Dutch oven or a slow cooker on the stovetop over medium-high heat. Brown the beef roast on all sides until nicely seared. Remove the beef from the pot and set aside.

3. In the same pot, add the chopped onion and minced garlic. Sauté until fragrant and golden.

4. Add the sliced carrots and celery to the pot. Cook for a few minutes, stirring occasionally.

5. Return the seared beef roast to the pot. Pour in the beef broth and red wine, followed by the tomato paste. Stir well to combine.

6. Add the bay leaves, dried thyme, and dried rosemary. Stir and bring the mixture to a simmer.

7. If using a Dutch oven, cover it and transfer it to a preheated oven at 325°F (160°C). Cook for about 3-4 hours until the beef is tender and easily shreds apart.

8. If using a slow cooker, transfer the beef and vegetable mixture to the slow cooker. Cook on low heat for 6-8 hours or on high heat for 4-6 hours.

9. About 30 minutes before serving, add the halved baby potatoes to the pot. Cook until the potatoes are fork-tender.

Once cooked, remove the bay leaves and shred the beef. Serve the slow-cooked pot roast stew hot, garnished with freshly chopped parsley. Enjoy with a slice of crusty bread.

5.2 Tender Braised Beef Stew with Red Wine
Ingredients:

- 2 pounds (900g) beef stew meat, cut into chunks
- Salt and pepper to taste
- 3 tablespoons olive oil
- 1 onion, chopped
- 3 cloves garlic, minced
- 2 carrots, peeled and sliced
- 2 parsnips, peeled and sliced
- 8 ounces (225g) mushrooms, quartered
- 2 tablespoons tomato paste
- 2 cups red wine
- 2 cups beef broth
- 2 bay leaves
- 1 teaspoon dried thyme
- 1 teaspoon dried rosemary
- Chopped fresh parsley for garnish

Instructions:

1. Season the beef stew meat with salt and pepper on all sides.
2. Heat the olive oil in a large Dutch oven or a slow cooker on the stovetop over medium-high heat. Brown the beef chunks on all sides until nicely seared. Remove the beef from the pot and set aside.
3. In the same pot, add the chopped onion and minced garlic. Sauté until fragrant and golden.
4. Add the sliced carrots, parsnips, and quartered mushrooms to the pot. Cook for a few minutes, stirring occasionally.
5. Return the seared beef chunks to the pot. Stir in the tomato paste, red wine, and beef broth.
6. Add the bay leaves, dried thyme, and dried rosemary. Stir and

bring the mixture to a simmer.

7. If using a Dutch oven, cover it and transfer it to a preheated oven at 325°F (160°C). Cook for about 2-3 hours until the beef is tender and the flavors have melded together.

8. If using a slow cooker, transfer the beef and vegetable mixture to the slow cooker. Cook on low heat for 6-8 hours or on high heat for 4-6 hours.

Once cooked, remove the bay leaves. Serve the tender braised beef stew with red wine hot, garnished with freshly chopped parsley. Pair it with mashed potatoes or crusty bread for a hearty meal.

5.3 Rustic Beef and Barley Stew
Ingredients:

- 1 pound (450g) beef stew meat, cut into chunks
- Salt and pepper to taste
- 2 tablespoons olive oil
- 1 onion, chopped
- 2 cloves garlic, minced
- 2 carrots, peeled and chopped
- 2 celery stalks, chopped
- 1 cup sliced mushrooms
- 1/2 cup pearl barley
- 4 cups beef broth
- 1 can (14 oz/400g) diced tomatoes
- 1 bay leaf
- 1 teaspoon dried thyme
- Chopped fresh parsley for garnish

Instructions:

1. Season the beef stew meat with salt and pepper on all sides.
2. Heat the olive oil in a large Dutch oven or a slow cooker on the stovetop over medium-high heat. Brown the beef chunks on all sides until nicely seared. Remove the beef from the pot and set aside.
3. In the same pot, add the chopped onion and minced garlic. Sauté until fragrant and golden.
4. Add the chopped carrots, celery, and sliced mushrooms to the pot. Cook for a few minutes, stirring occasionally.
5. Return the seared beef chunks to the pot. Stir in the pearl barley, beef broth, diced tomatoes, bay leaf, and dried thyme.
6. If using a Dutch oven, cover it and transfer it to a preheated oven at 325°F (160°C). Cook for about 2-3 hours until the beef

is tender and the barley is cooked.

7. If using a slow cooker, transfer the beef and vegetable mixture to the slow cooker. Cook on low heat for 6-8 hours or on high heat for 4-6 hours.

Once cooked, remove the bay leaf. Serve the rustic beef and barley stew hot, garnished with freshly chopped parsley. Enjoy this comforting stew on its own or with a side of crusty bread.

These comforting slow-cooked stews are perfect for colder days or when you want to enjoy the process of simmering flavors developing over time. In the next chapters, we'll explore lighter and healthier variations of beef stews, as well as quick and easy recipes for those busy days. Get ready to continue your culinary adventure!

Chapter 6: One-Pot Wonders

In this chapter, we'll explore the magic of one-pot wonders—delicious beef stews that come together in a single pot, making cleanup a breeze. These recipes are inspired by Mediterranean, Italian, and Southwestern flavors. Get ready to savor the Mediterranean-inspired beef and vegetable stew, indulge in the rich Italian-style tomato and beef stew, and enjoy the bold and spicy Southwestern beef and black bean stew.

6.1 Mediterranean-Inspired Beef and Vegetable Stew

Ingredients:

- 2 pounds (900g) beef stew meat, cut into chunks
- Salt and pepper to taste
- 3 tablespoons olive oil
- 1 onion, chopped
- 3 cloves garlic, minced
- 1 red bell pepper, chopped
- 1 zucchini, diced
- 1 eggplant, diced
- 1 can (14 oz/400g) diced tomatoes
- 1 cup beef broth
- 1 teaspoon dried oregano
- 1 teaspoon dried basil
- 1/2 teaspoon dried thyme
- 1/2 cup pitted black olives
- Chopped fresh parsley for garnish

Instructions:

1. Season the beef stew meat with salt and pepper on all sides.
2. Heat the olive oil in a large Dutch oven or a deep skillet over medium-high heat. Brown the beef chunks on all sides until

nicely seared. Remove the beef from the pot and set aside.

3. In the same pot, add the chopped onion and minced garlic. Sauté until fragrant and golden.
4. Add the red bell pepper, diced zucchini, and diced eggplant to the pot. Cook for a few minutes, stirring occasionally.
5. Return the seared beef chunks to the pot. Stir in the diced tomatoes, beef broth, dried oregano, dried basil, and dried thyme.
6. Bring the mixture to a simmer, then reduce the heat to low. Cover the pot and let it simmer for 1.5 to 2 hours until the beef is tender and the flavors have melded together.
7. Stir in the pitted black olives and cook for an additional 5 minutes.

Once cooked, adjust the seasoning if needed. Serve the Mediterranean-inspired beef and vegetable stew hot, garnished with freshly chopped parsley. Enjoy it with crusty bread or over a bed of couscous.

6.2 Italian-Style Tomato and Beef Stew
Ingredients:

- 2 pounds (900g) beef stew meat, cut into chunks
- Salt and pepper to taste
- 3 tablespoons olive oil
- 1 onion, chopped
- 3 cloves garlic, minced
- 2 carrots, peeled and chopped
- 2 celery stalks, chopped
- 1 can (14 oz/400g) crushed tomatoes
- 1 cup beef broth
- 1/2 cup red wine (optional)
- 2 teaspoons dried basil
- 1 teaspoon dried oregano
- 1/2 teaspoon dried rosemary
- Grated Parmesan cheese for garnish
- Chopped fresh basil for garnish

Instructions:

1. Season the beef stew meat with salt and pepper on all sides.
2. Heat the olive oil in a large Dutch oven or a deep skillet over medium-high heat. Brown the beef chunks on all sides until nicely seared. Remove the beef from the pot and set aside.
3. In the same pot, add the chopped onion and minced garlic. Sauté until fragrant and golden.
4. Add the chopped carrots and celery to the pot. Cook for a few minutes, stirring occasionally.
5. Return the seared beef chunks to the pot. Stir in the crushed tomatoes, beef broth, red wine (if using), dried basil, dried oregano, and dried rosemary.
6. Bring the mixture to a simmer, then reduce the heat to low.

Cover the pot and let it simmer for 1.5 to 2 hours until the beef is tender and the flavors have melded together.

Once cooked, adjust the seasoning if needed. Serve the Italian-style tomato and beef stew hot, garnished with grated Parmesan cheese and freshly chopped basil. Pair it with crusty bread or serve it over pasta for a hearty Italian meal.

6.3 Southwestern Beef and Black Bean Stew
Ingredients:

- 2 pounds (900g) beef stew meat, cut into chunks
- Salt and pepper to taste
- 3 tablespoons vegetable oil
- 1 onion, chopped
- 3 cloves garlic, minced
- 1 red bell pepper, chopped
- 1 green bell pepper, chopped
- 1 jalapeño pepper, seeded and chopped (optional)
- 1 can (14 oz/400g) diced tomatoes with green chilies
- 1 can (14 oz/400g) black beans, rinsed and drained
- 2 cups beef broth
- 1 teaspoon chili powder
- 1 teaspoon ground cumin
- 1/2 teaspoon smoked paprika
- Chopped fresh cilantro for garnish
- Sour cream and sliced green onions for garnish (optional)

Instructions:

1. Season the beef stew meat with salt and pepper on all sides.
2. Heat the vegetable oil in a large Dutch oven or a deep skillet over medium-high heat. Brown the beef chunks on all sides until nicely seared. Remove the beef from the pot and set aside.
3. In the same pot, add the chopped onion and minced garlic. Sauté until fragrant and golden.
4. Add the chopped red bell pepper, green bell pepper, and jalapeño pepper (if using) to the pot. Cook for a few minutes, stirring occasionally.
5. Return the seared beef chunks to the pot. Stir in the diced tomatoes with green chilies, black beans, beef broth, chili

powder, ground cumin, and smoked paprika.

6. Bring the mixture to a simmer, then reduce the heat to low. Cover the pot and let it simmer for 1.5 to 2 hours until the beef is tender and the flavors have melded together.

Once cooked, adjust the seasoning if needed. Serve the Southwestern beef and black bean stew hot, garnished with chopped fresh cilantro. Add a dollop of sour cream and sliced green onions on top, if desired. Enjoy it with warm tortillas or over cooked rice.

These one-pot wonders are not only delicious but also convenient, as they require minimal cleanup. In the next chapters, we'll explore lighter variations of beef stews and quick and easy recipes for those busy days. Get ready to continue your culinary journey with exciting flavors!

Chapter 7: Creative Variations

In this chapter, we'll dive into creative variations of beef stew that will tantalize your taste buds. Get ready to explore the smoky flavors of chipotle in the beef stew, savor the tanginess of balsamic vinegar, and indulge in a creamy mushroom and beef stew.

7.1 Smoky Chipotle Beef Stew

Ingredients:

- 2 pounds (900g) beef stew meat, cut into chunks
- Salt and pepper to taste
- 3 tablespoons vegetable oil
- 1 onion, chopped
- 3 cloves garlic, minced
- 1 red bell pepper, chopped
- 1 chipotle pepper in adobo sauce, chopped
- 1 can (14 oz/400g) diced tomatoes
- 2 cups beef broth
- 2 teaspoons smoked paprika
- 1 teaspoon ground cumin
- 1/2 teaspoon dried oregano
- Chopped fresh cilantro for garnish
- Lime wedges for serving

Instructions:

1. Season the beef stew meat with salt and pepper on all sides.
2. Heat the vegetable oil in a large Dutch oven or a deep skillet over medium-high heat. Brown the beef chunks on all sides until nicely seared. Remove the beef from the pot and set aside.
3. In the same pot, add the chopped onion and minced garlic.

Sauté until fragrant and golden.

4. Add the chopped red bell pepper and chipotle pepper to the pot. Cook for a few minutes, stirring occasionally.

5. Return the seared beef chunks to the pot. Stir in the diced tomatoes, beef broth, smoked paprika, ground cumin, and dried oregano.

6. Bring the mixture to a simmer, then reduce the heat to low. Cover the pot and let it simmer for 1.5 to 2 hours until the beef is tender and the flavors have melded together.

Once cooked, adjust the seasoning if needed. Serve the smoky chipotle beef stew hot, garnished with chopped fresh cilantro. Squeeze lime juice over each serving for an extra burst of flavor. Enjoy it with warm tortillas or rice.

7.2 Tangy Balsamic Beef Stew
Ingredients:

- 2 pounds (900g) beef stew meat, cut into chunks
- Salt and pepper to taste
- 3 tablespoons olive oil
- 1 onion, chopped
- 3 cloves garlic, minced
- 2 carrots, peeled and chopped
- 2 celery stalks, chopped
- 1 cup sliced mushrooms
- 2 tablespoons balsamic vinegar
- 1 can (14 oz/400g) crushed tomatoes
- 2 cups beef broth
- 1 teaspoon dried thyme
- 1/2 teaspoon dried rosemary
- Chopped fresh parsley for garnish

Instructions:

1. Season the beef stew meat with salt and pepper on all sides.
2. Heat the olive oil in a large Dutch oven or a deep skillet over medium-high heat. Brown the beef chunks on all sides until nicely seared. Remove the beef from the pot and set aside.
3. In the same pot, add the chopped onion and minced garlic. Sauté until fragrant and golden.
4. Add the chopped carrots, celery, and sliced mushrooms to the pot. Cook for a few minutes, stirring occasionally.
5. Return the seared beef chunks to the pot. Stir in the balsamic vinegar, crushed tomatoes, beef broth, dried thyme, and dried rosemary.
6. Bring the mixture to a simmer, then reduce the heat to low. Cover the pot and let it simmer for 1.5 to 2 hours until the beef

is tender and the flavors have melded together.

Once cooked, adjust the seasoning if needed. Serve the tangy balsamic beef stew hot, garnished with chopped fresh parsley. Pair it with crusty bread or mashed potatoes for a delightful meal.

7.3 Creamy Mushroom and Beef Stew
Ingredients:

- 2 pounds (900g) beef stew meat, cut into chunks
- Salt and pepper to taste
- 3 tablespoons butter
- 1 onion, chopped
- 3 cloves garlic, minced
- 1 pound (450g) cremini mushrooms, sliced
- 2 tablespoons all-purpose flour
- 1 cup beef broth
- 1 cup heavy cream
- 1 teaspoon dried thyme
- 1/2 teaspoon dried rosemary
- Chopped fresh parsley for garnish

Instructions:

1. Season the beef stew meat with salt and pepper on all sides.
2. In a large Dutch oven or a deep skillet, melt the butter over medium-high heat. Brown the beef chunks on all sides until nicely seared. Remove the beef from the pot and set aside.
3. In the same pot, add the chopped onion and minced garlic. Sauté until fragrant and golden.
4. Add the sliced cremini mushrooms to the pot. Cook for a few minutes until the mushrooms release their moisture and start to brown.
5. Sprinkle the flour over the mushrooms and stir to coat them evenly. Cook for an additional minute.
6. Return the seared beef chunks to the pot. Stir in the beef broth, heavy cream, dried thyme, and dried rosemary.
7. Bring the mixture to a simmer, then reduce the heat to low. Cover the pot and let it simmer for 1.5 to 2 hours until the beef

is tender and the flavors have melded together.

Once cooked, adjust the seasoning if needed. Serve the creamy mushroom and beef stew hot, garnished with chopped fresh parsley. Enjoy it with mashed potatoes or crusty bread.

These creative variations of beef stew will bring exciting flavors to your table. Next, we'll explore lighter options for those seeking a healthier twist on this classic dish. Get ready for some delicious and nutritious recipes!

Chapter 8: Light and Healthy Options

In this chapter, we'll explore light and healthy variations of beef stew that are perfect for those seeking nutritious options. Discover the flavors of a lean beef and vegetable stew, enjoy the goodness of quinoa and beef stew, and find a low-sodium beef stew recipe suitable for dietary restrictions.

8.1 Lean Beef and Vegetable Stew
Ingredients:

- 2 pounds (900g) lean beef stew meat, cut into chunks
- Salt and pepper to taste
- 1 tablespoon olive oil
- 1 onion, chopped
- 3 cloves garlic, minced
- 2 carrots, peeled and chopped
- 2 celery stalks, chopped
- 1 red bell pepper, chopped
- 1 zucchini, diced
- 1 can (14 oz/400g) diced tomatoes
- 2 cups beef broth (low-sodium, if preferred)
- 1 teaspoon dried thyme
- 1/2 teaspoon dried rosemary
- Chopped fresh parsley for garnish

Instructions:

1. Season the lean beef stew meat with salt and pepper on all sides.
2. Heat the olive oil in a large Dutch oven or a deep skillet over medium-high heat. Brown the beef chunks on all sides until nicely seared. Remove the beef from the pot and set aside.
3. In the same pot, add the chopped onion and minced garlic.

Sauté until fragrant and golden.

4. Add the chopped carrots, celery, red bell pepper, and diced zucchini to the pot. Cook for a few minutes, stirring occasionally.
5. Return the seared lean beef chunks to the pot. Stir in the diced tomatoes, beef broth, dried thyme, and dried rosemary.
6. Bring the mixture to a simmer, then reduce the heat to low. Cover the pot and let it simmer for 1.5 to 2 hours until the beef is tender and the flavors have melded together.

Once cooked, adjust the seasoning if needed. Serve the lean beef and vegetable stew hot, garnished with chopped fresh parsley. Enjoy this lighter version of beef stew packed with nutritious ingredients.

8.2 Quinoa and Beef Stew
Ingredients:

- 2 pounds (900g) beef stew meat, cut into chunks
- Salt and pepper to taste
- 1 tablespoon vegetable oil
- 1 onion, chopped
- 3 cloves garlic, minced
- 2 carrots, peeled and chopped
- 2 celery stalks, chopped
- 1 cup quinoa, rinsed
- 1 can (14 oz/400g) diced tomatoes
- 3 cups beef broth (low-sodium, if preferred)
- 1 teaspoon dried thyme
- 1/2 teaspoon dried rosemary
- Chopped fresh parsley for garnish

Instructions:

1. Season the beef stew meat with salt and pepper on all sides.
2. Heat the vegetable oil in a large Dutch oven or a deep skillet over medium-high heat. Brown the beef chunks on all sides until nicely seared. Remove the beef from the pot and set aside.
3. In the same pot, add the chopped onion and minced garlic. Sauté until fragrant and golden.
4. Add the chopped carrots and celery to the pot. Cook for a few minutes, stirring occasionally.
5. Return the seared beef chunks to the pot. Stir in the rinsed quinoa, diced tomatoes, beef broth, dried thyme, and dried rosemary.
6. Bring the mixture to a simmer, then reduce the heat to low. Cover the pot and let it simmer for 1.5 to 2 hours until the beef is tender and the flavors have melded together.

Once cooked, adjust the seasoning if needed. Serve the quinoa and beef stew hot, garnished with chopped fresh parsley. This nutritious stew combines the goodness of quinoa and beef for a satisfying and healthy meal.

8.3 Low-Sodium Beef Stew for Dietary Restrictions

Ingredients:

- 2 pounds (900g) beef stew meat, cut into chunks
- Salt-free seasoning blend to taste
- 1 tablespoon olive oil
- 1 onion, chopped
- 3 cloves garlic, minced
- 2 carrots, peeled and chopped
- 2 celery stalks, chopped
- 1 potato, peeled and diced
- 1 can (14 oz/400g) low-sodium diced tomatoes
- 2 cups low-sodium beef broth
- 1 teaspoon dried thyme
- 1/2 teaspoon dried rosemary
- Chopped fresh parsley for garnish

Instructions:

1. Season the beef stew meat with salt-free seasoning blend on all sides.
2. Heat the olive oil in a large Dutch oven or a deep skillet over medium-high heat. Brown the beef chunks on all sides until nicely seared. Remove the beef from the pot and set aside.
3. In the same pot, add the chopped onion and minced garlic. Sauté until fragrant and golden.
4. Add the chopped carrots, celery, and diced potato to the pot. Cook for a few minutes, stirring occasionally.
5. Return the seared beef chunks to the pot. Stir in the low-sodium diced tomatoes, low-sodium beef broth, dried thyme, and dried rosemary.
6. Bring the mixture to a simmer, then reduce the heat to low. Cover the pot and let it simmer for 1.5 to 2 hours until the beef

is tender and the flavors have melded together.

Once cooked, adjust the seasoning if needed. Serve the low-sodium beef stew hot, garnished with chopped fresh parsley. This recipe is suitable for those with dietary restrictions who need to limit their sodium intake.

Enjoy these light and healthy variations of beef stew, packed with wholesome ingredients and flavor. In the next chapter, we'll explore time-saving recipes for those busy days when you need a quick and delicious meal.

Chapter 9: Global Stews

In this chapter, we'll take a culinary journey and explore stews from around the world. Experience the rich flavors of an Irish-inspired beef and Guinness stew, indulge in the savory Japanese-style beef sukiyaki stew, and savor the hearty Brazilian feijoada, a black bean and beef stew.

9.1 Irish-Inspired Beef and Guinness Stew
Ingredients:

- 2 pounds (900g) beef stew meat, cut into chunks
- Salt and pepper to taste
- 3 tablespoons vegetable oil
- 1 onion, chopped
- 3 cloves garlic, minced
- 2 carrots, peeled and chopped
- 2 celery stalks, chopped
- 4 potatoes, peeled and diced
- 1 can (14 oz/400g) diced tomatoes
- 2 cups beef broth
- 1 cup Guinness stout
- 1 tablespoon tomato paste
- 1 tablespoon Worcestershire sauce
- 2 teaspoons dried thyme
- Chopped fresh parsley for garnish

Instructions:

1. Season the beef stew meat with salt and pepper on all sides.
2. Heat the vegetable oil in a large Dutch oven or a deep skillet over medium-high heat. Brown the beef chunks on all sides until nicely seared. Remove the beef from the pot and set aside.

3. In the same pot, add the chopped onion and minced garlic. Sauté until fragrant and golden.
4. Add the chopped carrots, celery, and diced potatoes to the pot. Cook for a few minutes, stirring occasionally.
5. Return the seared beef chunks to the pot. Stir in the diced tomatoes, beef broth, Guinness stout, tomato paste, Worcestershire sauce, and dried thyme.
6. Bring the mixture to a simmer, then reduce the heat to low. Cover the pot and let it simmer for 2 to 3 hours until the beef is tender and the flavors have melded together.

Once cooked, adjust the seasoning if needed. Serve the Irish-inspired beef and Guinness stew hot, garnished with chopped fresh parsley. Enjoy it with crusty bread for a hearty meal.

9.2 Japanese-Style Beef Sukiyaki Stew
Ingredients:

- 1 pound (450g) beef sirloin, thinly sliced
- 1 tablespoon vegetable oil
- 1 onion, sliced
- 2 cups Napa cabbage, chopped
- 1 cup shiitake mushrooms, sliced
- 1 cup sliced carrots
- 1 cup sliced green onions
- 1/4 cup soy sauce
- 2 tablespoons mirin (Japanese sweet rice wine)
- 2 tablespoons sugar
- 1 cup beef broth
- 1 block of tofu, cut into cubes
- 4 ounces (113g) glass noodles (optional)
- Sesame seeds for garnish

Instructions:

1. Heat the vegetable oil in a large skillet or a sukiyaki pan over medium-high heat.
2. Add the sliced beef sirloin to the skillet and cook until browned. Remove the beef from the skillet and set aside.
3. In the same skillet, add the sliced onion, Napa cabbage, shiitake mushrooms, sliced carrots, and sliced green onions. Sauté for a few minutes until the vegetables start to soften.
4. In a bowl, mix together the soy sauce, mirin, sugar, and beef broth. Pour the mixture into the skillet with the vegetables.
5. Add the tofu cubes to the skillet and gently stir to combine.
6. If using glass noodles, soak them in hot water until softened, then add them to the skillet.
7. Cook the stew for a few more minutes until the flavors have

melded together and the vegetables are tender.

Once cooked, transfer the Japanese-style beef sukiyaki stew to a serving dish. Garnish with sesame seeds and serve it hot. Enjoy this flavorful and comforting Japanese dish.

9.3 Brazilian Feijoada: A Black Bean and Beef Stew
Ingredients:

- 1 pound (450g) beef stew meat, cut into chunks
- 1 pound (450g) smoked sausage, sliced
- 1 onion, chopped
- 4 cloves garlic, minced
- 2 cups cooked black beans
- 2 cups beef broth
- 1 can (14 oz/400g) diced tomatoes
- 2 bay leaves
- Salt and pepper to taste
- Chopped fresh cilantro for garnish
- Cooked rice and orange slices for serving

Instructions:

1. In a large Dutch oven or a deep skillet, brown the beef stew meat and sliced smoked sausage over medium-high heat. Remove them from the pot and set aside.
2. In the same pot, add the chopped onion and minced garlic. Sauté until fragrant and golden.
3. Return the browned beef stew meat and smoked sausage to the pot. Add the cooked black beans, beef broth, diced tomatoes, and bay leaves.
4. Season with salt and pepper to taste. Stir well to combine.
5. Bring the mixture to a boil, then reduce the heat to low. Cover the pot and let the feijoada simmer for 1.5 to 2 hours until the beef is tender and the flavors have melded together.

Once cooked, adjust the seasoning if needed. Serve the Brazilian feijoada hot, garnished with chopped fresh cilantro. Accompany it with cooked rice and orange slices for an authentic Brazilian experience.

Embark on a global culinary adventure with these delightful stews from Ireland, Japan, and Brazil. The next chapter will focus on quick and easy stews that can be prepared in a flash for those busy weeknights. Get ready for delicious recipes that save time without compromising on flavor.

Chapter 10: Stews with a Twist

In this chapter, we'll explore unique and flavorful stews that offer a delightful twist to traditional recipes. Indulge in a beer-braised beef stew with caramelized onions, savor the Mediterranean-inspired beef stew with olives and feta, and experience the enticing flavors of an Asian-inspired ginger and soy-infused beef stew.

10.1 Beer-Braised Beef Stew with Caramelized Onions

Ingredients:

- 2 pounds (900g) beef stew meat, cut into chunks
- Salt and pepper to taste
- 3 tablespoons vegetable oil
- 2 onions, thinly sliced
- 3 cloves garlic, minced
- 2 carrots, peeled and chopped
- 2 celery stalks, chopped
- 1 cup mushrooms, sliced
- 2 tablespoons tomato paste
- 2 cups beef broth
- 1 bottle of dark beer (such as stout or porter)
- 1 tablespoon Worcestershire sauce
- 1 teaspoon dried thyme
- Chopped fresh parsley for garnish

Instructions:

1. Season the beef stew meat with salt and pepper on all sides.
2. Heat 2 tablespoons of vegetable oil in a large Dutch oven or a deep skillet over medium-high heat. Brown the beef chunks on all sides until nicely seared. Remove the beef from the pot and

set aside.

3. In the same pot, add the remaining tablespoon of vegetable oil and sliced onions. Cook the onions over medium heat, stirring occasionally, until they caramelize and turn golden brown.
4. Add the minced garlic, chopped carrots, chopped celery, and sliced mushrooms to the pot. Sauté for a few minutes until the vegetables start to soften.
5. Stir in the tomato paste and cook for another minute.
6. Return the seared beef chunks to the pot. Pour in the beef broth, dark beer, Worcestershire sauce, and dried thyme. Stir well to combine.
7. Bring the mixture to a simmer, then reduce the heat to low. Cover the pot and let it simmer for 2 to 3 hours until the beef is tender and the flavors have melded together.

Once cooked, adjust the seasoning if needed. Serve the beer-braised beef stew with caramelized onions hot, garnished with chopped fresh parsley. The rich flavors of the beer and caramelized onions add a delightful twist to this comforting stew.

10.2 Mediterranean-Inspired Beef Stew with Olives and Feta

Ingredients:

- 2 pounds (900g) beef stew meat, cut into chunks
- Salt and pepper to taste
- 3 tablespoons olive oil
- 1 onion, chopped
- 3 cloves garlic, minced
- 1 red bell pepper, sliced
- 1 yellow bell pepper, sliced
- 1 zucchini, diced
- 1 can (14 oz/400g) diced tomatoes
- 1 cup beef broth
- 1 teaspoon dried oregano
- 1 teaspoon dried basil
- 1/2 cup pitted Kalamata olives
- 1/2 cup crumbled feta cheese
- Chopped fresh parsley for garnish

Instructions:

1. Season the beef stew meat with salt and pepper on all sides.
2. Heat the olive oil in a large Dutch oven or a deep skillet over medium-high heat. Brown the beef chunks on all sides until nicely seared. Remove the beef from the pot and set aside.
3. In the same pot, add the chopped onion and minced garlic. Sauté until fragrant and golden.
4. Add the sliced red bell pepper, sliced yellow bell pepper, and diced zucchini to the pot. Cook for a few minutes, stirring occasionally.
5. Return the seared beef chunks to the pot. Stir in the diced tomatoes, beef broth, dried oregano, and dried basil.
6. Bring the mixture to a simmer, then reduce the heat to low.

Cover the pot and let it simmer for 2 to 3 hours until the beef is tender and the flavors have melded together.

7. Once cooked, adjust the seasoning if needed. Stir in the Kalamata olives.

Serve the Mediterranean-inspired beef stew hot, garnished with crumbled feta cheese and chopped fresh parsley. The combination of olives and feta adds a unique and delicious twist to this hearty stew.

10.3 Asian-Inspired Ginger and Soy-Infused Beef Stew
Ingredients:

- 2 pounds (900g) beef stew meat, cut into chunks
- Salt and pepper to taste
- 3 tablespoons vegetable oil
- 1 onion, chopped
- 3 cloves garlic, minced
- 2 carrots, peeled and sliced
- 1 red bell pepper, sliced
- 1 cup snow peas
- 1/4 cup soy sauce
- 2 tablespoons oyster sauce
- 1 tablespoon hoisin sauce
- 1 tablespoon grated fresh ginger
- 2 cups beef broth
- 1 teaspoon cornstarch (optional, for thickening)
- Sliced green onions for garnish

Instructions:

1. Season the beef stew meat with salt and pepper on all sides.
2. Heat the vegetable oil in a large Dutch oven or a deep skillet over medium-high heat. Brown the beef chunks on all sides until nicely seared. Remove the beef from the pot and set aside.
3. In the same pot, add the chopped onion and minced garlic. Sauté until fragrant and golden.
4. Add the sliced carrots, sliced red bell pepper, and snow peas to the pot. Cook for a few minutes, stirring occasionally.
5. Return the seared beef chunks to the pot. Stir in the soy sauce, oyster sauce, hoisin sauce, grated ginger, and beef broth.
6. Bring the mixture to a simmer, then reduce the heat to low. Cover the pot and let it simmer for 2 to 3 hours until the beef is

tender and the flavors have melded together.

7. If desired, thicken the stew by mixing cornstarch with a little water to make a slurry. Stir the slurry into the stew and cook for an additional 5 minutes until thickened.

Once cooked, adjust the seasoning if needed. Serve the Asian-inspired ginger and soy-infused beef stew hot, garnished with sliced green onions. The ginger and soy flavors add a delightful twist to this comforting and aromatic stew.

These unique and flavorful stews with a twist are sure to impress your taste buds. In the next chapter, we'll explore vegetarian and vegan options for those who prefer plant-based dishes. Get ready to discover delicious and hearty vegetable stews that are both satisfying and nutritious.

Chapter 11: Vegetarian/Vegan Beef Stew Alternatives

In this chapter, we'll explore satisfying and flavorful alternatives to traditional beef stew for those following a vegetarian or vegan diet. Discover the deliciousness of a hearty vegetable stew with a meatless beef substitute, indulge in a vegan lentil and vegetable stew with a beef-like texture, and savor the rich flavors of a mushroom and root vegetable stew that provides a meaty taste.

11.1 Hearty Vegetable Stew with Meatless Beef Substitute

Ingredients:

- 2 tablespoons olive oil
- 1 onion, chopped
- 3 cloves garlic, minced
- 2 carrots, peeled and chopped
- 2 celery stalks, chopped
- 1 red bell pepper, chopped
- 1 cup chopped mushrooms
- 1 cup diced potatoes
- 1 cup diced butternut squash
- 1 can (14 oz/400g) diced tomatoes
- 4 cups vegetable broth
- 2 cups meatless beef substitute (such as textured vegetable protein or tempeh)
- 2 teaspoons dried thyme
- Salt and pepper to taste
- Chopped fresh parsley for garnish

Instructions:

1. Heat the olive oil in a large pot over medium heat. Add the

chopped onion and minced garlic. Sauté until fragrant and golden.

2. Add the chopped carrots, chopped celery, chopped red bell pepper, chopped mushrooms, diced potatoes, and diced butternut squash to the pot. Cook for a few minutes, stirring occasionally.

3. Stir in the diced tomatoes and vegetable broth. Bring the mixture to a boil, then reduce the heat to low.

4. Add the meatless beef substitute to the pot, along with the dried thyme, salt, and pepper. Stir well to combine.

5. Cover the pot and let the stew simmer for about 30 minutes, or until the vegetables are tender and the flavors have melded together.

6. Adjust the seasoning if needed. Serve the hearty vegetable stew hot, garnished with chopped fresh parsley. The meatless beef substitute adds a satisfying and protein-rich element to this delicious vegetarian stew.

11.2 Vegan Lentil and Vegetable Stew with Beef-Like Texture

Ingredients:

- 2 tablespoons olive oil
- 1 onion, chopped
- 3 cloves garlic, minced
- 2 carrots, peeled and chopped
- 2 celery stalks, chopped
- 1 cup chopped bell peppers (any color)
- 1 cup diced tomatoes
- 1 cup dried brown lentils, rinsed
- 4 cups vegetable broth
- 2 cups meatless beef crumbles (made from soy or other plant-based proteins)
- 2 teaspoons smoked paprika
- 1 teaspoon cumin
- Salt and pepper to taste
- Chopped fresh cilantro for garnish

Instructions:

1. Heat the olive oil in a large pot over medium heat. Add the chopped onion and minced garlic. Sauté until fragrant and golden.
2. Add the chopped carrots, chopped celery, and chopped bell peppers to the pot. Cook for a few minutes, stirring occasionally.
3. Stir in the diced tomatoes, dried brown lentils, and vegetable broth. Bring the mixture to a boil, then reduce the heat to low.
4. Add the meatless beef crumbles to the pot, along with the smoked paprika, cumin, salt, and pepper. Stir well to combine.
5. Cover the pot and let the stew simmer for about 30 minutes, or until the lentils are tender and the flavors have melded together.

6. Adjust the seasoning if needed. Serve the vegan lentil and vegetable stew hot, garnished with chopped fresh cilantro. The meatless beef crumbles provide a beef-like texture to this satisfying and protein-packed stew.

11.3 Mushroom and Root Vegetable Stew for a Meaty Flavor

Ingredients:

- 2 tablespoons vegetable oil
- 1 onion, chopped
- 3 cloves garlic, minced
- 8 ounces (225g) mushrooms, sliced
- 2 carrots, peeled and chopped
- 2 parsnips, peeled and chopped
- 2 turnips, peeled and chopped
- 2 potatoes, peeled and chopped
- 2 cups vegetable broth
- 1 cup red wine (optional)
- 2 tablespoons tomato paste
- 2 teaspoons soy sauce
- 1 teaspoon dried thyme
- Salt and pepper to taste
- Chopped fresh parsley for garnish

Instructions:

1. Heat the vegetable oil in a large pot over medium heat. Add the chopped onion and minced garlic. Sauté until fragrant and golden.

2. Add the sliced mushrooms to the pot. Cook for a few minutes, stirring occasionally, until the mushrooms release their moisture and start to brown.

3. Stir in the chopped carrots, parsnips, turnips, and potatoes. Cook for another few minutes, allowing the vegetables to slightly soften.

4. Pour in the vegetable broth and red wine (if using). Add the tomato paste, soy sauce, dried thyme, salt, and pepper. Stir well to combine.

5. Cover the pot and let the stew simmer for about 30 minutes, or until the vegetables are tender and the flavors have melded together.

6. Adjust the seasoning if needed. Serve the mushroom and root vegetable stew hot, garnished with chopped fresh parsley. The combination of mushrooms and root vegetables provides a meaty flavor that satisfies the palate.

These vegetarian and vegan beef stew alternatives offer a range of delicious options for those looking to enjoy a hearty and flavorful meal without the use of meat. In the next chapter, we'll delve into the realm of side dishes and accompaniments that perfectly complement beef stew. Get ready to enhance your dining experience with delectable sides that elevate the flavors of the main dish.

Chapter 12: Sides and Accompaniments

In this chapter, we'll explore a variety of mouthwatering side dishes and accompaniments that perfectly complement your beef stew. From fluffy mashed potatoes to buttery biscuits and freshly baked crusty bread, these additions will elevate your dining experience and enhance the flavors of the main dish.

12.1 Fluffy Mashed Potatoes

Ingredients:

- 2 pounds (900g) russet potatoes, peeled and cut into chunks
- 4 tablespoons unsalted butter
- 1/2 cup milk (or dairy-free milk alternative)
- Salt and pepper to taste
- Chopped fresh chives or parsley for garnish (optional)

Instructions:

1. Place the potato chunks in a large pot and cover them with cold water. Add a pinch of salt to the water.
2. Bring the water to a boil and cook the potatoes until tender when pierced with a fork, usually around 15-20 minutes.
3. Drain the cooked potatoes and return them to the pot.
4. Add the butter and milk to the pot with the potatoes.
5. Mash the potatoes using a potato masher or a fork until smooth and creamy.
6. Season with salt and pepper to taste.

Transfer the fluffy mashed potatoes to a serving bowl and garnish with chopped fresh chives or parsley if desired. Serve alongside your beef stew to enjoy the perfect pairing of creamy potatoes and savory meat.

12.2 Buttery Biscuits
Ingredients:

- 2 cups all-purpose flour
- 2 teaspoons baking powder
- 1/2 teaspoon salt
- 1/2 cup unsalted butter, cold and cubed
- 3/4 cup milk (or dairy-free milk alternative)
- 2 tablespoons melted butter for brushing

Instructions:

1. Preheat your oven to 425°F (220°C) and line a baking sheet with parchment paper.
2. In a large bowl, whisk together the flour, baking powder, and salt.
3. Add the cold, cubed butter to the bowl. Use a pastry cutter or your fingers to cut the butter into the dry ingredients until the mixture resembles coarse crumbs.
4. Gradually pour in the milk while stirring the mixture until it comes together into a dough.
5. Transfer the dough onto a lightly floured surface and knead it gently for a minute or two until it becomes smooth.
6. Roll out the dough to a thickness of about 1/2 inch (1.25 cm). Use a biscuit cutter or a glass to cut out biscuit rounds.
7. Place the biscuit rounds on the prepared baking sheet, leaving a little space between each.
8. Brush the tops of the biscuits with melted butter.
9. Bake in the preheated oven for 12-15 minutes or until the biscuits are golden brown and cooked through.
10. Remove from the oven and let the biscuits cool slightly before serving. These buttery biscuits are perfect for sopping up the flavorful gravy of your beef stew.

12.3 Freshly Baked Crusty Bread
Ingredients:

- 4 cups bread flour
- 2 teaspoons instant yeast
- 2 teaspoons salt
- 2 cups warm water

Instructions:

1. In a large mixing bowl, combine the bread flour, instant yeast, and salt.
2. Gradually add the warm water to the bowl while stirring with a wooden spoon until the dough comes together.
3. Turn the dough out onto a lightly floured surface and knead it for about 8-10 minutes until it becomes smooth and elastic.
4. Place the dough in a lightly greased bowl, cover it with a clean kitchen towel, and let it rise in a warm place for about 1-2 hours or until it has doubled in size.
5. Preheat your oven to 450°F (230°C) and place a baking stone or baking sheet inside to heat up.
6. Punch down the risen dough and shape it into a round or oval loaf.
7. Place the shaped dough onto a baking sheet or directly onto the preheated baking stone.
8. Score the top of the loaf with a sharp knife to create decorative slashes.
9. Bake in the preheated oven for 25-30 minutes or until the crust is golden brown and the bread sounds hollow when tapped on the bottom.
10. Remove the freshly baked crusty bread from the oven and let it cool on a wire rack before slicing. Serve thick slices of warm bread alongside your beef stew for a comforting and satisfying

meal.

These delightful side dishes and accompaniments will elevate your beef stew to new heights. The fluffy mashed potatoes, buttery biscuits, and freshly baked crusty bread will add depth and variety to your meal, providing the perfect balance of textures and flavors. In the next chapter, we'll explore delectable ways to repurpose any leftover beef stew into equally delicious dishes. Get ready to transform your leftovers into culinary delights!

Chapter 13: Perfect Pairings: Wine and Beer Suggestions

In this chapter, we'll explore the art of pairing beverages with your beef stew. Whether you prefer wine, beer, or non-alcoholic options, we have recommendations to enhance your dining experience and elevate the flavors of your stew.

13.1 Wine Recommendations for Beef Stews

Choosing the right wine can greatly complement the rich flavors and textures of your beef stew. Here are some wine recommendations to enhance your culinary experience:

Full-bodied red wines: opt for bold red wines such as Cabernet Sauvignon, Merlot, Syrah (Shiraz), or Malbec. These wines have robust flavors and tannins that pair well with the hearty nature of beef stew.

Zinfandel: Zinfandel is a versatile red wine that offers fruity notes and spice, making it a great match for beef stew.

Red blends: Consider red blends that incorporate a mix of grape varieties. These blends often provide a balance of fruitiness, tannins, and complexity that complement the flavors of the stew.

Remember, personal taste preferences vary, so feel free to explore different wine options and find the one that pleases your palate the most.

13.2 Beer Pairings for a Robust Stew Experience

Beer can be an excellent companion to beef stew, offering a refreshing contrast and complementary flavors. Here are some beer styles that pair well with robust stews:

Stout: Rich and dark stouts, such as Guinness or oatmeal stout, bring a velvety texture and flavors of roasted malt and coffee, which harmonize with the hearty flavors of beef stew.

Brown Ale: The toasty, caramel notes of a brown ale complement the savory flavors of the stew, adding depth to the overall experience.

Belgian Dubbel: With its malty sweetness, hints of spice, and mild bitterness, a Belgian dubbel can bring an interesting contrast and complexity to your beef stew.

Experiment with different beer styles and brands to find the one that best suits your taste preferences and complements the flavors of your stew.

13.3 Non-Alcoholic Beverage Suggestions

If you prefer non-alcoholic beverages or are looking for alternatives, there are plenty of options to enjoy with your beef stew:

Sparkling Water with Citrus: The effervescence and subtle citrus flavors of sparkling water can cleanse the palate and refresh your taste buds between bites.

Iced Tea: A glass of iced tea, whether classic black tea or herbal varieties, provides a soothing and thirst-quenching accompaniment to the hearty stew.

Apple Cider: The natural sweetness and fruity flavors of apple cider can provide a pleasant contrast to the savory notes of the stew.

Vegetable or Beef Broth: Sip on a warm cup of vegetable or beef broth to complement the flavors of the stew and add an extra layer of richness.

Feel free to explore different non-alcoholic options and find the ones that suit your taste preferences and complement your beef stew.

Choosing the right beverage to accompany your beef stew can enhance the overall dining experience. Whether you prefer wine, beer, or non-alcoholic options, these recommendations will help you find the perfect pairing. In the next chapter, we'll dive into the world of delectable desserts that can be enjoyed after a satisfying bowl of beef stew. Get ready to indulge in sweet treats that will leave a lasting impression!

Chapter 14: Leftover Magic: Repurposing Stews

Leftovers are a great opportunity to get creative in the kitchen and transform your beef stew into new and exciting dishes. In this chapter, we'll explore three delicious ways to repurpose your leftover stew, turning them into mouthwatering creations.

14.1 Beef Stew Pot Pie

Ingredients:

- Leftover beef stew
- Pie crust (store-bought or homemade)
- 1 egg, beaten (for egg wash)

Instructions:

1. Preheat your oven to the temperature specified on the pie crust packaging or to 375°F (190°C) if using homemade pie crust.
2. Take your leftover beef stew and transfer it to a baking dish or individual ramekins, filling them about three-quarters of the way.
3. Roll out the pie crust on a floured surface to fit the top of your baking dish or ramekins.
4. Place the pie crust over the stew, pressing the edges to seal.
5. Cut a few slits on the top of the pie crust to allow steam to escape.
6. Brush the pie crust with beaten egg for a golden finish.
7. Place the baking dish or ramekins on a baking sheet and bake in the preheated oven for about 30-35 minutes, or until the crust is golden brown and the filling is bubbling.
8. Remove from the oven and let it cool for a few minutes before serving. Enjoy the comforting and hearty beef stew pot pie!

14.2 Stuffed Bell Peppers with Leftover Stew
Ingredients:

- Leftover beef stew
- Bell peppers (any color)
- Shredded cheese (optional)

Instructions:

1. Preheat your oven to 375°F (190°C).
2. Cut the tops off the bell peppers and remove the seeds and membranes.
3. Fill each bell pepper with leftover beef stew, packing it in tightly.
4. Place the stuffed bell peppers in a baking dish and cover with foil.
5. Bake in the preheated oven for 30-35 minutes or until the bell peppers are tender.
6. Remove the foil and sprinkle shredded cheese on top if desired.
7. Return to the oven and bake for an additional 5-10 minutes, or until the cheese is melted and bubbly.
8. Remove it from the oven and let it cool for a few minutes before serving. Enjoy the flavorful and colorful stuffed bell peppers!

14.3 Beef Stew Nachos
Ingredients:

- Leftover beef stew
- Tortilla chips
- Shredded cheese
- Sliced jalapeños
- Diced tomatoes
- Sour cream
- Chopped fresh cilantro

Instructions:

1. Preheat your oven to 375°F (190°C).
2. Spread a layer of tortilla chips on a baking sheet or oven-safe dish.
3. Spoon leftover beef stew evenly over the tortilla chips.
4. Sprinkle shredded cheese, sliced jalapeños, and diced tomatoes over the stew.
5. Bake in the preheated oven for about 10-15 minutes or until the cheese has melted and the nachos are heated through.
6. Remove from the oven and let it cool for a few minutes.
7. Garnish with dollops of sour cream and chopped fresh cilantro.
8. Serve the beef stew nachos as a flavorful and satisfying snack or appetizer.

These creative and delicious recipes will transform your leftover beef stew into new and exciting dishes. Whether you choose to make a comforting pot pie, stuffed bell peppers, or flavorful nachos, these repurposed meals will impress your taste buds. In the next chapter, we'll explore the art of garnishing and presenting your beef stew to create visually stunning and appetizing dishes. Get ready to take your culinary creations to the next level!

Chapter 15: Time-Saving Tips and Tricks

Preparing a delicious beef stew doesn't have to be a time-consuming task. In this chapter, we'll explore time-saving tips and tricks to help you make the most of your cooking experience. Whether you're looking for quick preparation techniques, want to learn how to freeze and reheat stew for later, or need ideas for making ahead on busy days, we've got you covered.

15.1 Quick Preparation Techniques

When you're short on time but still crave a comforting bowl of beef stew, these quick preparation techniques will come in handy:

opt for pre-cut stew meat: Look for pre-cut stew meat at your local grocery store or butcher. This saves you time on cutting and trimming the beef, allowing you to jump straight into the cooking process.

Use a pressure cooker: Pressure cookers are excellent for reducing cooking time while still producing tender and flavorful results. The high-pressure environment speeds up the cooking process, making it ideal for busy days.

Prep ingredients in advance: Take some time during the weekend or your free time to chop the vegetables, measure out the spices, and store them in labeled containers or resealable bags. This way, when it's time to make the stew, you can simply grab the prepped ingredients and get cooking.

15.2 Freezing and Reheating Stew for Later

If you find yourself with leftover stew or want to prepare a batch in advance for future meals, freezing and reheating the stew properly is key. Follow these steps for successful freezing and reheating:

Allow the stew to cool completely: Before freezing the stew, let it cool to room temperature to prevent condensation and ice crystals from forming.

Portion the stew: Divide the stew into individual or family-sized portions based on your needs. This makes it easier to thaw and reheat the desired amount.

Use freezer-safe containers or bags: Transfer the stew portions into freezer-safe containers or resealable bags, making sure to leave some room for expansion.

Label and date: Properly label each container or bag with the contents and the date it was frozen.

Freeze the stew: Place the labeled containers or bags in the freezer, ensuring they are stored upright to prevent leaks.

Reheat properly: When you're ready to enjoy the frozen stew, thaw it overnight in the refrigerator. Reheat on the stovetop over low heat or in a microwave, stirring occasionally until heated through. Make sure the internal temperature reaches 165°F (74°C) for food safety.

15.3 Making Ahead for Busy Days

To stay ahead of the game on busy days, try these make-ahead tips for your beef stew:

Prep the stew ingredients the night before: Chop the vegetables, trim the meat, and measure out the spices the night before. Store them in separate containers in the refrigerator, so all you have to do the next day is combine the ingredients and cook.

Slow cooker convenience: If you own a slow cooker or Crock-Pot, take advantage of its convenience. Prep the ingredients the night before, refrigerate them in a slow cooker insert, and simply place it in the slow cooker base the next morning. Set it to cook on low throughout the day, and return home to a delicious, ready-to-serve stew.

Cook in large batches: When you have the time, consider cooking a large batch of stew. Portion it out into individual servings or family-sized containers and refrigerate or freeze for future meals. This way, you'll have homemade stew on hand whenever you need a quick and satisfying meal.

By implementing these time-saving tips and tricks, you can enjoy the flavors of a delicious beef stew even on your busiest days. Whether you're utilizing quick preparation techniques, freezing and reheating stew for later, or making ahead for convenience, these strategies will help you savor a hearty meal with minimal effort. In the next chapter, we'll dive into the art of garnishing and presenting your beef stew to make it visually stunning and appetizing. Get ready to elevate your stew to new heights!

Chapter 16: Comforting Stews for Every Season

Beef stew is a versatile dish that can be enjoyed throughout the year. In this chapter, we'll explore comforting stews tailored to each season, ensuring you have delicious options no matter the time of year. From lighter spring-inspired stews to chilled options for summer and hearty choices for fall and winter, we've got your seasonal stew cravings covered.

16.1 Lighter Spring-Inspired Beef Stews

As the weather warms up and fresh produce becomes abundant, lighter and refreshing beef stews can be a delightful choice. Here are some ideas to capture the essence of spring in your stew:

Spring Vegetable Beef Stew: Incorporate seasonal vegetables like asparagus, peas, and baby carrots into your stew. Their vibrant colors and delicate flavors will add a touch of freshness to the dish.

Lemon Herb Beef Stew: Brighten up your stew with the zest and juice of fresh lemons. Add a medley of herbs like thyme, rosemary, and parsley for a burst of springtime flavors.

Spring Greens and Beef Stew: Include nutritious greens such as spinach, kale, or Swiss chard to your stew. They not only add a vibrant color but also provide a healthy dose of vitamins and minerals.

16.2 Summery Chilled Beef Stew Options

When the heat of summer arrives, chilled beef stews can offer a refreshing and satisfying meal. Consider these ideas for a cool and delightful summer stew experience:

Gazpacho-Inspired Beef Stew: Take inspiration from the classic chilled tomato soup and create a gazpacho-inspired beef stew. Blend fresh tomatoes, cucumbers, bell peppers, and other summer vegetables into a flavorful base for your stew. Add tender beef chunks to create a refreshing and cooling dish.

Cold Asian Beef Noodle Salad: Transform your beef stew into a chilled noodle salad with an Asian twist. Toss cold cooked noodles, sliced beef, crisp vegetables, and a tangy dressing together for a light and satisfying summertime meal.

Mediterranean Chilled Beef Stew: Infuse your stew with Mediterranean flavors by adding ingredients like olives, feta cheese, cucumber, and mint. Serve it chilled for a delightful and flavorful summer dish.

16.3 Hearty Fall and Winter Beef Stews

As the temperature drops and the leaves start to change, hearty and warming beef stews are perfect for fall and winter. Embrace the cozy vibes with these comforting options:

Slow-Cooked Beef and Root Vegetable Stew: Take advantage of the bountiful harvest of fall by including root vegetables like carrots, parsnips, and potatoes in your stew. Slow cook the ingredients for hours, allowing the flavors to meld together into a rich and comforting dish.

Spiced Pumpkin and Beef Stew: Harness the flavors of autumn by incorporating pumpkin or butternut squash into your stew. The natural sweetness and warm spices like cinnamon, nutmeg, and cloves will create a cozy and aromatic experience.

Hearty Beef and Barley Stew: As the weather gets colder, a beef and barley stew becomes the ultimate comfort food. The tender beef, hearty barley, and robust flavors from herbs and spices will keep you warm and satisfied on chilly winter nights.

By tailoring your beef stews to each season, you can enjoy the comforting flavors of this classic dish year-round. Whether you're savoring lighter and refreshing stews in spring, chilled options for a cool summer, or hearty creations in fall and winter, these seasonal variations will keep your taste buds satisfied. In the next chapter, we'll dive into the art of garnishing and presenting your beef stew to create visually stunning and appetizing dishes. Get ready to elevate your stew to new heights!

Chapter 17: Stews from Around the World

Exploring global flavors is an exciting way to elevate your beef stew repertoire. In this chapter, we'll embark on a culinary journey and discover three delicious stews from different corners of the world. From an African-inspired beef and peanut stew to a Spanish-style beef and chorizo stew, and a Caribbean-style beef stew with plantains, get ready to indulge in international flavors right in your own kitchen.

17.1 African-Inspired Beef and Peanut Stew

Experience the rich and vibrant flavors of Africa with this mouthwatering beef and peanut stew. Here's how to create this delicious fusion:

Ingredients:

- 2 pounds (900g) beef stew meat, cubed
- 1 onion, finely chopped
- 3 garlic cloves, minced
- 1 tablespoon grated fresh ginger
- 1 teaspoon ground coriander
- 1 teaspoon ground cumin
- 1/2 teaspoon cayenne pepper (adjust to taste)
- 1 cup peanut butter
- 4 cups beef broth
- 2 cups diced tomatoes
- 2 cups chopped sweet potatoes
- 1 cup chopped carrots
- Salt and pepper to taste
- Fresh cilantro, for garnish

Instructions:

1. In a large pot or Dutch oven, heat some oil over medium heat. Add the beef stew meat and brown it on all sides. Remove the meat and set it aside.
2. In the same pot, add the chopped onion, minced garlic, and grated ginger. Sauté until the onion becomes translucent and fragrant.
3. Add the ground coriander, ground cumin, and cayenne pepper to the pot. Stir well to coat the onions and spices.
4. Return the browned beef stew meat to the pot. Add the peanut butter and stir until it melts and coats the meat.
5. Pour in the beef broth and diced tomatoes. Stir to combine all the ingredients.
6. Add the chopped sweet potatoes and carrots to the pot. Season with salt and pepper to taste.
7. Bring the stew to a boil, then reduce the heat to low. Cover the pot and simmer for about 1.5 to 2 hours, or until the beef is tender and the flavors have melded together.
8. Serve the African-inspired beef and peanut stew hot, garnished with fresh cilantro. It pairs well with steamed rice or crusty bread.

17.2 Spanish-Style Beef and Chorizo Stew

Transport your taste buds to the vibrant streets of Spain with this hearty and flavorful beef and chorizo stew. Here's how to create this tantalizing dish:

Ingredients:

- 1 pound (450g) beef stew meat, cubed
- 1 tablespoon olive oil
- 1 onion, diced
- 3 garlic cloves, minced
- 1 red bell pepper, diced
- 1 chorizo sausage, sliced
- 1 teaspoon smoked paprika
- 1 teaspoon dried oregano
- 1 teaspoon ground cumin
- 1 can (14 ounces) diced tomatoes
- 2 cups beef broth
- Salt and pepper to taste
- Fresh parsley, for garnish

Instructions:

1. In a large pot or Dutch oven, heat the olive oil over medium heat. Add the beef stew meat and brown it on all sides. Remove the meat and set it aside.
2. In the same pot, add the diced onion, minced garlic, and diced red bell pepper. Sauté until the vegetables are softened.
3. Add the sliced chorizo sausage to the pot. Cook for a few minutes until it releases its flavorful oils.
4. Return the browned beef stew meat to the pot. Sprinkle the smoked paprika, dried oregano, and ground cumin over the ingredients. Stir well to coat everything with the spices.
5. Pour in the diced tomatoes and beef broth. Season with salt and

pepper to taste.

6.　Bring the stew to a boil, then reduce the heat to low. Cover the pot and simmer for about 1.5 to 2 hours, or until the beef is tender and the flavors have melded together.

7.　Serve the Spanish-style beef and chorizo stew hot, garnished with fresh parsley. It pairs beautifully with crusty bread or a side of saffron-infused rice.

17.3 Caribbean-Style Beef Stew with Plantains

Indulge in the tropical flavors of the Caribbean with this delightful beef stew featuring sweet and savory plantains. Here's how to create this Caribbean-inspired dish:

Ingredients:

- 1.5 pounds (680g) beef stew meat, cubed
- 2 tablespoons vegetable oil
- 1 onion, chopped
- 3 garlic cloves, minced
- 1 red bell pepper, diced
- 1 green bell pepper, diced
- 2 ripe plantains, peeled and sliced
- 1 teaspoon ground allspice
- 1 teaspoon dried thyme
- 1 teaspoon paprika
- 1 can (14 ounces) coconut milk
- 1 cup beef broth
- Salt and pepper to taste
- Fresh cilantro, for garnish

Instructions:

1. In a large pot or Dutch oven, heat the vegetable oil over medium heat. Add the beef stew meat and brown it on all sides. Remove the meat and set it aside.
2. In the same pot, add the chopped onion, minced garlic, diced red bell pepper, and diced green bell pepper. Sauté until the vegetables are softened.
3. Add the sliced plantains to the pot and cook for a few minutes until they start to caramelize.
4. Return the browned beef stew meat to the pot. Sprinkle the ground allspice, dried thyme, and paprika over the ingredients.

Stir well to coat everything with the spices.

5. Pour in the coconut milk and beef broth. Season with salt and pepper to taste.

6. Bring the stew to a boil, then reduce the heat to low. Cover the pot and simmer for about 1.5 to 2 hours, or until the beef is tender and the flavors have melded together.

7. Serve the Caribbean-style beef stew with plantains hot, garnished with fresh cilantro. It pairs wonderfully with steamed rice or traditional Caribbean rice and peas.

By exploring stews from around the world, you can broaden your culinary horizons and experience a diverse range of flavors and ingredients. In the next chapter, we'll dive into the art of garnishing and presenting your beef stew to create visually stunning and appetizing dishes. Get ready to take your stew to new heights!

Chapter 18: Family-Friendly Stews

When it comes to feeding the whole family, it's important to have delicious and kid-approved beef stew recipes on hand. In this chapter, we'll explore family-friendly stews that are sure to please even the pickiest eaters. We'll also include healthy variations to ensure your little ones are getting their essential nutrients. Lastly, we'll discover how to transform leftover stew into flavorful sandwiches and wraps, perfect for lunchboxes or quick meals on the go.

18.1 Kid-Approved Beef Stew Recipes

Getting kids to enjoy their meals can sometimes be a challenge, but with these kid-approved beef stew recipes, you'll have them asking for seconds:

Cheesy Beef and Potato Stew: Add a kid-friendly twist to your beef stew by incorporating chunks of melted cheese and diced potatoes. The creamy texture and familiar flavors will make this stew a hit with the little ones.

Mini Meatball Stew: Transform your beef stew into a fun and interactive meal by shaping the beef into bite-sized meatballs. Kids will love scooping up the meatballs with their spoons and savoring them with the flavorful stew broth.

Sweet and Savory Teriyaki Beef Stew: Infuse your beef stew with a hint of sweetness by adding a teriyaki-inspired sauce. The combination of tender beef, colorful vegetables, and a sticky teriyaki glaze will entice even the fussiest eaters.

18.2 Healthy Variations for Picky Eaters

For picky eaters who are more reluctant to try new flavors and textures, these healthy variations of beef stew can help introduce them to new ingredients and provide a balanced meal:

Hidden Veggie Beef Stew: Sneak in nutritious vegetables by finely chopping or pureeing them before adding them to the stew. Carrots, bell peppers, and zucchini are excellent choices that can go unnoticed by picky eaters.

Cauliflower and Beef Stew: Replace some of the potatoes or other starchy vegetables in the stew with cauliflower florets. This adds a boost of vitamins and fiber while maintaining a familiar texture.

Quinoa and Vegetable Beef Stew: Incorporate cooked quinoa into your beef stew for an added protein and nutrient punch. The small grains blend well with the stew, providing a texture that picky eaters may find more appealing.

18.3 Stew-Inspired Sandwiches and Wraps

Transforming leftover stew into sandwiches and wraps is a great way to enjoy the flavors in a portable and convenient format. Here are a few ideas to turn your beef stew into delectable handheld meals:

Beef Stew Sliders: Place a scoop of leftover beef stew between mini burger buns or slider rolls. Add a slice of cheese, pickles, and any desired condiments for a delicious and hearty slider experience.

Stew-Stuffed Pita Pockets: Fill pita pockets with leftover beef stew and top with shredded lettuce, diced tomatoes, and a dollop of yogurt or tzatziki sauce. This creates a flavorful and satisfying handheld meal.

Tortilla Wrap with Beef Stew: Spread a tortilla with cream cheese or your favorite spread, then add a generous portion of leftover beef stew. Roll it up and slice into pinwheels for a lunchtime favorite.

By incorporating kid-approved beef stew recipes, offering healthy variations, and transforming leftovers into sandwiches and wraps, you can create family-friendly meals that everyone will enjoy. In the next chapter, we'll explore the art of garnishing and presenting your beef stew to make it visually stunning and appetizing. Get ready to elevate your stew to new heights!

Chapter 19: Festive and Special Occasion Stews

Stews aren't just for everyday meals—they can also be the star of festive gatherings and special occasions. In this chapter, we'll explore a variety of stews that are perfect for adding a touch of elegance and celebration to your table. From holiday-inspired beef stew with festive flavors to sophisticated options for dinner parties, as well as celebratory stews for birthdays or anniversaries, these recipes will make your special occasions truly memorable.

19.1 Holiday-Inspired Beef Stew with Festive Flavors

During the holiday season, delight your guests with a beef stew that captures the essence of the festivities. Here's a recipe that incorporates festive flavors:

Cranberry-Glazed Beef Stew: Add a tangy and sweet twist to your beef stew by incorporating a cranberry glaze. The combination of tender beef, seasonal vegetables, and the vibrant burst of cranberries will evoke the holiday spirit and create a memorable dining experience.

19.2 Elegant Beef Stew for Dinner Parties

When hosting a dinner party, impress your guests with a sophisticated and flavorful beef stew. Consider the following options:

Red Wine and Herb Beef Stew: Elevate your beef stew by using a rich and robust red wine as the base. The wine adds depth of flavor and complements the tender beef and aromatic herbs. Serve this stew with crusty bread and a glass of red wine for an elegant dining experience.

Truffle-Infused Beef Stew: Indulge in the luxurious and earthy flavors of truffles by incorporating truffle oil or truffle paste into your beef stew. This elegant twist will elevate the stew to a whole new level of sophistication.

19.3 Celebratory Stews for Birthdays or Anniversaries

Marking a special milestone calls for a celebratory stew that is worthy of the occasion. Consider the following options for birthdays or anniversaries:

Champagne and Mushroom Beef Stew: Add a touch of elegance and celebration by using champagne as a flavor enhancer in your beef stew. The bubbles and delicate notes of champagne pair beautifully with mushrooms, creating a refined and memorable dish.

Lobster and Beef Stew: For a truly indulgent and luxurious celebration, combine tender beef with succulent lobster in a creamy stew. This surf-and-turf combination is perfect for special occasions and will leave a lasting impression on your guests.

By incorporating festive flavors, preparing elegant stews for dinner parties, and creating celebratory stews for birthdays or anniversaries, you can infuse your special occasions with culinary delights. In the next chapter, we'll explore the art of garnishing and presenting your beef stew to make it visually stunning and appetizing. Get ready to impress your guests with not only the flavors but also the presentation of your stews!

Chapter 20: Sweet Endings: Desserts with Stew Ingredients

Who says stew ingredients are only reserved for savory dishes? In this final chapter, we'll explore how you can incorporate the flavors and ingredients from your beef stew into delicious and surprising desserts. From rich chocolate and beef-infused desserts to fruity compotes with a stew twist, and even decadent ice cream sundaes with stew toppings, these sweet creations will provide a delightful and unexpected conclusion to your culinary journey.

20.1 Rich Chocolate and Beef-Infused Dessert

Combine the richness of chocolate with the savory notes of beef for a dessert that will leave your taste buds intrigued and satisfied. Try this recipe for a unique and indulgent treat:

Beef and Chocolate Truffles: Create a decadent treat by combining finely chopped beef and dark chocolate ganache. Roll the mixture into small truffle balls, then coat them in cocoa powder, powdered sugar, or crushed nuts. The unexpected combination of savory beef and sweet chocolate will surprise and delight your palate.

20.2 Fruity Compote with Beef Stew Twist

Add a twist to traditional fruit compotes by incorporating elements from your beef stew. This unexpected combination will bring a delightful contrast of flavors to your dessert. Here's a recipe to try:

Spiced Fruit Compote with Beef Reduction: Prepare a fragrant fruit compote using a variety of seasonal fruits such as apples, pears, and berries. To add a beef stew twist, reduce some of the flavorful beef broth from your stew and incorporate it into the compote. The savory undertones of the beef reduction will add depth and complexity to the sweet and tangy fruits.

20.3 Decadent Ice Cream Sundae with Stew Toppings

Elevate your favorite ice cream sundae by incorporating toppings inspired by your beef stew. These indulgent additions will take your dessert to the next level. Here's a delightful suggestion:

Caramelized Fruit and Beef Syrup Sundae: Take caramelized fruits, such as bananas or apples, and combine them with a rich syrup made from reducing the beef stew broth. Drizzle the caramelized fruit and beef syrup over a scoop of your favorite ice cream, and top it off with whipped cream, crushed nuts, and a cherry. The sweet and savory combination will create a memorable and indulgent dessert experience.

By venturing into the world of desserts with stew ingredients, you can surprise your guests with unexpected flavors and unique culinary creations. Remember to let your imagination run wild and experiment with different combinations to create sweet endings that will leave a lasting impression. Enjoy the journey of exploring the diverse possibilities of beef stew in both savory and sweet realms!

Conclusion

Congratulations on completing this culinary journey through the "Pressure Cooker Beef Stew Cookbook"! Throughout this book, we have explored the wonderful world of beef stews and discovered a wide range of recipes that cater to different tastes, preferences, and occasions. From classic and exotic flavors to light and healthy options, one-pot wonders, and even sweet endings, we've covered a diverse array of stew recipes that are sure to impress your family, friends, and guests.

By harnessing the power of pressure cooking, you can create tender, flavorful, and hearty beef stews in a fraction of the time compared to traditional cooking methods. We have also provided essential tips, safety guidelines, and guidance on selecting the best ingredients to ensure your cooking experience is enjoyable and successful.

Whether you're a seasoned chef or a beginner in the kitchen, this cookbook is designed to inspire and empower you to create delicious and satisfying meals. The variations in content and recipes offer a wide range of flavors and styles, ensuring that there's something for everyone.

Remember, cooking is an art that allows you to express your creativity and share your love for food with others. Don't be afraid to experiment, adapt, and make these recipes your own. Feel free to adjust the seasonings, add your favorite ingredients, and explore new flavor combinations to suit your personal taste.

Now armed with the knowledge and recipes from this cookbook, you can confidently embark on your culinary adventures and create mouthwatering pressure cooker beef stews that will become family favorites and cherished dishes for years to come.

So, fire up your pressure cooker, gather your ingredients, and let your imagination run wild as you dive into the world of pressure cooker beef stews. Enjoy the process, savor the flavors, and share the joy of these hearty and comforting meals with your loved ones. Happy cooking!

www.ingramcontent.com/pod-product-compliance
Lightning Source LLC
Chambersburg PA
CBHW020628160726
47991CB00002B/950